MW00588187

Prayer is the Master Key
Revised Edition

Raising Prophetic Intercessors in
Times Like These.

SARAH MORGAN

Copyright © 2016 SARAH MORGAN
All rights reserved.
ISBN:978-0-9859690-5-9

MORGAN PUBLISHING
The Feet of a Ready Writer

Prayer is the Master Key: Raising Prophetic Prayer
Warriors in Times Like These
Published by Morgan Publishing
P.O. Box 470047
Los Angeles, CA 90047
(323)-295-1501
www.womenofvisionla.org
www.facebook.com/officialwomenofvisionla
www.twitter.com/womenofvisionla
www.periscope.com/womenofvisionla

All rights reserved. No part of this book may be
reproduced or transmitted in any form or by any means
without written permission from the author.

ISBN 978-0-9859690-5-9

Cover Design by Dee Shervell
Editing and typesetting by Fresh Reign Publishing

Copyright © 2016 by Sarah Morgan

Printed in USA by 48HrBooks (www.48HrBooks.com)

Dedication

But if they be prophets and if the Word of the Lord be with them now make intercession to the Lord of Host, that the vessels which are left in the house of the Lord, and in the house of the kings of Judah, and at Jerusalem, go not to Babylon (captivity) Jeremiah 27:18.

I dedicate this to:
To all the days-men and days-women who stand betwixt (Job 9:33).

To all the watchmen and watch women on the wall who have refused to hold their peace or remain silent until righteous fills the earth (Isaiah 62:6).

To all the pleaders who are ceaselessly reasoning with God (Isaiah 43:26).

To all the mourning women, the weeping women who have taken up a waling for us, and are teaching their daughters how to wail (Jeremiah 9:17-20)

To the fathers (Apostles) who have travailed and Zion has brought forth her children (Isaiah 66:8).

3

To the prophetic Anna's (mothers in Zion), who have not departed from the temple – but have served with prayers and fasting night and day – until redemption comes to this generation and generations to come (Luke 2:37).

To Zion who has travailed and has brought forth her children (Isaiah 66:8).

To the precious Holy Spirit, our Chief Intercessors, who make intercessions for us with groaning's which cannot be uttered (Romans 8:26).

To all the "Prayer Warriors" – past, present and future.

And above all, to our Chief Apostle, Great High Priest, Always and Forever, Intercessor, Jesus Christ, the Son of the Living God.

I salute you. Thank you.
Prophetess Sarah Morgan

Table of Contents

Acknowledgements

Apostle Paul wrote in 1 Corinthians 4:15, *"For though ye have ten thousand instructors in Christ yet ye have not many Fathers: for in Christ Jesus I have begotten you through the gospel."*

I extend my heartfelt gratitude to my husband, the Honorable Bishop Peter Morgan, for your example of prayer and intercession. Your life of prayer has truly challenged, motivated, inspired and stimulated my life. To Pastor Ravi thanks for teaching the importance of early morning am hour of prayer.

To all the prayer warriors here a Vision International Ministries: Kenneth Brown, Joel Morgan, Dawn Gray, Etta Jenkins, Mama Brewer, Mama Westmoreland, Minette Young, Videla Wallar, Comfort Innis, Mamma Stella Besse, Annie Umoh and your team – and to all those not mentioned. I appreciate you – especially for those 5:00 a.m. prayers.

To Dr. Minnie Claiborne, Sister Claressa Hawkins, Sister Florence La Rue, Sister Shirley Brown Sister Dawn Gray, Sister Fiona Gebreselassie and Bishop Morgan – thank you for financially making this project happen.

To my covenant sisters: Fidelia Collin-Wood Williams, Pastor Jemima Amoako, Prophetess Marcia

Graves, Prophetess Veronica Coffey and Pastor Josephine Kyambadde, I thank God for you being in my life. To dear Sister Carol Ellis, thank you for enduring and taking up the challenge of transcribing this awesome book. WE DID IT!

To my elder Sister Joanne Montgomery, thank you, thank, thank you, for typing all the correspondence letters and all that this entailed. And of course, I cannot forget Pastor Candace Cole Kelley and the staff at Cole Publishing – you are truly God sent. Thank you for bringing this project from vision to reality. Thank you again, Vision family. Forget the rest, you are simply the best!

I love you all,
Pastor Sarah Morgan

Forward

By Bishop Peter Morgan

Sarah, from the very moment that I met her until the Lord Himself gave her to me for a wife, I sensed strongly within me that she was a choice vessel of God; a woman with a fine and well-balanced intellect. She is a woman with unclouded focus and perception and with a firm and unshaken determination and resolve to tread deeper and deeper in her relationship with God. Today, I am greatly honored and imperatively thankful to God for the opportunity to pen the foreword for this great and life-transforming book.

Anyone who desires to put behind them a superficial prayer life will find this book a priceless treasure.

"But, this kind does not go out except by prayer and fasting," declared Jesus (Matthew 17:21) AMP.

Prayer and fasting is the bedrock of every major Move of God in the life of a nation, a church, or an individual. There are certain problems in our lives that would not be resolved so easily except through serious and consistent prayers and fasting.

You can request anything from God if it is in His Word. If you can only pray and fast according to the

Word of God, your victory is just a prayer away. Jesus our Lord and Savior, spent most of His time, during His earthly mission in prayer. He literally began with prayer and concluded His assignment with prayer. His last words on the cross before he gave up the ghost were prayerful declarations. Prayer was one of the three major pillars that held together the ministry of Jesus, the other two being the Word and the Holy Spirit.

Whenever men have been willing to deny themselves their night's sleep so that they might abandon themselves to prayer, revival has followed. God is looking for real intercessors. God does not expect us to carry on the ministry of Jesus with less equipment than he had. We need to set our sights high and refuse the traditions of men who say that it is impossible to do as Jesus instructed us: *"Pray without ceasing"* (I Thessalonians 5:17). Do not stop praying until you receive the answer. Why? Because God wants to hear your prayers an answer them. Why? Because God wants to hear your prayers and answer them. "O you who hear; to all flesh will come" (Psalm 65:2).

It is reported about John G. Lake, a great apostle of his time, a man without compromise, of how one day in his ministry he saw a vision. In that vision Lake saw an angel take him through the Book of Acts speaking to him these words: "This is Pentecost as God gave it through the heart of Jesus. Strive for this. Contend for this. Teach the people to pray for this. For this, and this alone, will meet the necessity of the human heart, and

10

this alone will have the power to overcome the forces darkness." As the angel departed, he said: "Pray, pray, pray. Teach the people to pray. Prayer and prayer alone, much prayer, persistent prayer, is the door of entrance into the heart of God.

Satan truly exists as an active force in the world. He is alive and evil. He is a dark enemy agent: a terrible, mysterious, fearsome reality; a lying spirit, perverted and enemy number one. The devil, the enemy of God and His people is a being of malignity, sophistication, and treachery; a spirit who is seducing modern men and women with drugs, pornography, sexual promiscuity, immorality, rebellion, materialism and the occult.

Whole nations have fallen under Satan's grip. Modern man relies too much on psychology, psychiatry, and sociology to explain the phenomenon of evil, and because of it, he loses his conception of a supernatural power of wickedness. The only real answer to the overwhelming evil and darkness that exist in our word is **PRAYER.**

Prayer, when offered rightly, can do whatever God can do. Prayer brings revelation, vision and knowledge. Prayer saves time, but does not take away time. Prayer moves God and prayer outlives those who pray. Prayerlessness is sin. Any time we fail to pray, we sin against God. The root of most human failures is prayerlessness. God has used His handmaiden, the Rev. Sarah Morgan to educate us about prayer and what prayer can do. The points, facts, truths, and insights about prayer, unfolded for us by Sarah, are *invaluable*. These facts, truths, when vigorously and persistently applied by the businessman, educator, lawyer, politician, housewife, pastor, student, Christian or even the non-Christian, I can guarantee, will yield positive and lasting results. Prayer is indeed the master key, the only key that can unlock the doors to hidden treasures, physical and spiritual.

Bishop W. Peter Morgan
Founder and President
Vision International Ministries
Los Angeles, CA
U.S.A.

Prayer is the Master Key

Raising Prophetic Intercessors In Times Like These

Chapter One
The Throne Room Invitation

What:	You are invited into the Throne Room of God.
When:	Continually.
Prerequisite:	Sanctify yourself with fasting, prayer and the Word of God.
Purpose:	This room is used for prayer, repentance, interceding, parga-ing, shaphat-ing, and supplication.

Beloved,

Did you know that you have been extended a personal invitation from God to be His Prophetic Intercessor? Do not let the title intimidate you, it simply means that God wants you to pray His Word.

And God's Word is Prophetic. He speaks those things that be not, as though they were (Romans 4:17), and encourages us, His people, to speak the Word over our lives and anticipate present and future impact.

The Latin root word of intercession is intercedere which means "to go between"; "to stand in the gap", or "to intervene between two parties with a view towards reconciling differences." The Hebrew word for intercession is parga which means "strike the mark." When you are an intercessor, you are called to parga; you are called to "strike the mark" and, due to the seriousness of our assignments, we cannot afford to miss! We need to pray targeted or specific prayers aimed at getting the needed results.

As intercessors, we are called to be spiritual snipers! We are on assignment for God. Our spiritual eyes should be sharp like those of the eagle and we should see beyond the natural into the spiritual realm. This means the intercessor is able to see beyond the surface (i.e. people with fancy suits, clothes, superior education, top careers, lots of influence and money) right into the heart of the matter.

Snipers need to have good eyesight and a steady trigger finger. They are not easily distracted by movement in the target area. Where does this type of fighting happen you may ask? The word of God invites us to a battle ground where we can intercede:

Let us come boldly to the Throne of grace, that we may obtain mercy and find grace to help in time of trouble" *(Hebrews 4:16).*

It is in the Throne Room that we are able to pray and able to speak God's Word concerning our lives, our situations, and our nation.

Guess what happens when you pray the Word? According to Isaiah 55:11 "*So shall my word be that goeth forth out of my mouth: it shall not return unto me void, but it shall accomplish that which I please, and it shall prosper in the thing whereto I sent it*". God promises that if we pray His Word, it will not return unto Him void, but it will prosper in the thing for which He sent it. Glory to God! That is exciting! In other words, when we pray God's word, He says, "I'm obligated to fulfill my Word in the sovereign manner that I choose."

Many of you reading this book may ask yourself, "What or who is a prophetic intercessor?" Simply put, a prophetic intercessor is a man or woman, boy or girl, who prays God's Word regarding various situations bringing about future impact, restoration, and healing. Yes, prophetic intercession affects people, places, and things. Jesus was our great Intercessor on earth. In John 17:1-26, He interceded on behalf of the believers and those that had not yet heard the Gospel of their salvation. He interceded on behalf of the disciples that they would be one, even as He and the father are one. Jesus is our great intercessor who still sits at the right hand of the Father making intercession for the believer.

In every dispensation of life, God has always used an intercessor to stand in the gap between Heaven and

Earth – making requests unto Him on behalf of His people and His will.

Who does God call for this type of task? Generally speaking, He uses plain old ordinary people like you and me. Further, He calls for those that love and honor Him; those who hate wickedness and shun evil. You must also have a love for His Word and embrace His Precepts and Laws.

Now, that sounds easy enough. However, when we carefully examine the people of God in history, we find only a faithful few that would stand on the wall; a faithful few that would intercede on behalf of the people according to God's leading.

Let's consider God's search for an intercessor in the book of Ezekiel:

> *"So I sought for a man among them who would make a wall, and stand in the gap before me on behalf of the land, that I should not destroy it; but I found no one"* (Ezekiel 22:30).

God is still calling for Prophetic Intercessors to assist in bringing about the transformation, reconciliations and healing that God has ordained for today. Will it be said by God in the twenty-first century, *"I sought for those that would pray, seek my face and petition me on behalf of the land, but found no one?"*

Beloved, know that Prayer is the Master Key! God has given us a Master Key which is the weapon of

Prayer. This key has no limits and it will open all the doors of our needs, requests, petitions and interventions.

I desire to share all that God has poured into me over the last several years regarding the need for Prophetic Intercessors. My prayer is that your life will be blessed and that you too will allow the intercessor to rise up in you; that you will pray until heaven opens and the gates of hell are shut up in your family and in your nation!

Chapter 1 Review

The Throne Room Invitation

1. Prophetic Intercession is ~~the~~ _a person/ intercessor_ who prays God's _Word_ into various situations that would bring about future order, restoration, and healing.

2. Prophetic Intercession is for (choose one):
   a. Prophets only
   b. Preachers and Teachers
   c. Whoever will
   d. Other:_____

3. The Latin root for intercession means "to go _between_", "to stand in the _Gap_____", or "to intervene between two _parties_____with a view towards reconciling differences."

4. "So I sought for a _Man_ among them who would make a wall, and stand in the _gap_____before me on behalf of the land, that I should not destroy it; but I found _no one_" (Ezekiel 22:30).

JOURNALING

MY THRONE ROOM EXPERIENCE

Reflect on the way you spend time with the Lord.
What needs to change?

Studying His Word,
devotions, Praise,
Worship, Praying.

Praying: a specific
Target for my family,
Church, Pastors, nation
healing

Pray different types
of Prayers, Do not
Pray admist.

Chapter 2

The Keys to Intercession

Keith rushed to his car after having his annual checkup at the doctor. He received an urgent message from his wife. Her water had broken and she was ready to go in the ambulance to the hospital to deliver their first son. Keith tried to put his key in the door of his car, but it would not work. He kept trying and finally he noticed he was using his house key.

Have you ever tried to open a door of intercession but felt you didn't have the right key with which to approach the throne? In this chapter, God has given me some specific keys to share with you.

In Chapter 1, we received a personal invitation from the King of Glory to enter into His Throne Room to stand in the gap for our loved ones, families, communities, churches, and nations. Intercessory prayer is a high calling and an honorable assignment. With every assignment in life, you must pursue the proper steps to achieve the intended outcome.

A **key** is a device that is used to operate a lock (such as to lock or unlock it). A **master key** can open many different types of locks. In order to Access Kingdom Authority it requires that you acquire Kingdom Keys. Jesus told Peter in **Matthew 16:19** *"And I will give unto*

A K A

21

thee the Keys of the Kingdom of heaven: and whatsoever thou shalt bind on earth shall be bound in heaven: and whatsoever thou shalt loose on earth shall be loosed in heaven."

A key is also an instrument that gives you access. It is an indicator, a pointer, a sign, a cue, a solution. Access is having the ability or right to approach something or someone, it permits you to enter, or to exit a place, or grants permission to communicate with someone. It is being permitted into a restricted area. It is a means of approaching or entering a place.

Keys also mean having access to classified material or sensitive information that you and others are not privy to. Access is the right, the opportunity, or ability to approach or enter a privileged place. To have access means you have passed through protocols, gates and doors and have attained clearance. Access means you have some connectivity with someone of influence that is authorized to endorse and approve your accessibility while others are standing outside. Access is a personal privilege based on relationship. **Matthew 6:33**- *But seek ye first the kingdom of God, and His righteousness; and all these things shall be added unto you.* Keys give you access and unrestricted admission, admittance, and entry.

Prayer is the Master Key. As a key is an instrument designed to turn a lock and unlock a door, prayer will unlock potential, prayer will unlock success and Prayer will unlock destiny. It is the Master Key to Gods Divine will for your life. Prayer will unlock your

22

purpose. It will give you access to realms and dimensions you would otherwise not be privy to or be able to enter into. Prayer will unlock joy, peace, and tranquility. Prayer is an aroma that touches every aspect of life, and we carry that smell into every area including the Church. Prayer will unlock Revelation and secrets of the kingdom; it will unlock mysteries and enigmas of the spirit realm, propelling you into destiny.

In this Chapter we examine five important keys to effective intercession. This not an exhaustive list, but I find these to be fundamental and, in my opinion, the most important:

1. **Be Specific:** When you need something from God and you are an intercessor, you do not go before Him and say just anything, don't be generic, ambiguous or elusive.

   Hebrews 4:16

   *"Let us therefore come boldly unto the **throne** of grace, that we may obtain mercy, and find grace to help in time of need."*

   Intercessors come boldly yet humbly before the throne of God which is also the throne of grace and make specific requests according to covenant promises.

2. **Identify the promise according to scripture:** Put God in remembrance of His Word. As an intercessor, you will plead the case of another

before the throne of God. *"And God said that there was no man, and wondered that there was no intercessor"* Isaiah 59:16a. God is seeking for someone that will remind Him of His promises, His covenant and His prophetic word; someone that will stand between God and man. Isaiah 43:26 (KJV) *"26 Put me in remembrance: let us plead together: declare thou, that thou mayest be justified."* According to one person's count, there are 3,573 promises in the bible. The word promise itself occurs over 50 times in the King James Version of the Bible.

2 Corinthians 1:20, *"For all the **promises** of God in him are yea, and in him Amen, unto the glory of God by us."*

3. **Fast:** People of God, when you are a Spiritual Sniper you cannot afford to eat all the time. Certain situations will require us to turn our plates down and our faces to the wall. Throughout history, God has called on His people to humble themselves through fasting and prayer. Fasting is a spiritual key that God uses to advance His kingdom, change the destiny of nations, spark revival, and bring victory in people's lives. There is something powerful that happens when we voluntarily humble ourselves, seek God's will, and agree

24

with Him for His purposes to be fulfilled. **Mark 9:29** "And he said unto them, This kind can come forth by nothing, but by prayer and **fasting**."

One example is Queen Esther who understood this third key and was a woman of intercession. She fearlessly faced her would-be enemy, the king, in the Throne Room of prayer with the key of fasting.

In the book of Esther, the fourth chapter, verses 15-16 says,

"Then Esther bade them return Mordecai this answer, go, gather together all the Jews that are present in Shushan, and fast ye for me, and neither eat nor drink three days, night or day: I also and my maidens will fast likewise; and so will I go unto the King, which is not according to the law; and if I perish, I perish."

And we, too, would do well to follow her example. We should never go into uncertain territory filled with self-confidence, but rather we should seek humbly the favor and power of God. There may be obstacles in our way that will never be moved until we fast and pray. When we come out of the wilderness of intercession, we can be confident in God's finished work and our testimony will be, *"not*

25

by might, not by power but by my Spirit saith the Lord" Zachariah 4:6.

4. **Supplication:** Sometimes intercessory prayer will cause you to cry before the Lord. In Jeremiah 9:1, crises out,

"Oh that my head were waters, and mine eyes a fountain of tears that I might weep day and night for the slain of the daughters of my people."

Supplication comes from the Latin verb supplicare, which means "to plead humbly." It means to petition or entreat someone in power for help or a favor.

1 Kings 8:30 *"And hearken thou to the **supplication** of thy servant, and of thy people Israel, when they shall pray toward this place: and hear thou in heaven thy dwelling place: and when thou hearest, forgive."*

1 Timothy 2:1 "I exhort therefore, that, first of all, supplications, prayers, intercessions, and giving of thanks, be made for all men;"

Who has God placed in your life that has had you weeping? Is it a son, a husband or wife? Is it our youth that are dying senseless deaths? Is it shepherds that have scattered God's sheep? What has you weeping? Something should have you weeping if you are a child of the King.

5. **P.U.S.H – Pray Until Something Happens:**
The intercessor realized that consistency is necessary to answered prayer. We have to be consistent, refusing to stop until we get an answer. Sometimes we pray for a day or two and when we do not see results, we are tempted to give up. The spirit of fear would then say to you, "Does God really want you to have that? Who are you to ask that of God? Are you really worthy of that breakthrough after all you've done?"

Isaiah 62:1 *"For Zion's sake will I not hold my peace, and for Jerusalem's sake I will not rest, until the righteousness thereof go forth as brightness, and the salvation thereof as a lamp that burneth."*

Luke 18:1 *"And he spake a parable unto them to this end, that men ought **always** to pray, and not to faint;"*

The devil is a liar, and so is his mother-in-law! The enemy will try to distract you and sometimes you will fall down, but just remember that the Bible says in Micah 7:8, *"When I fall, I shall arise."* When you fall there is a lifting up. Don't stop praying; keep your focus and P.U.S.H!

You are steps away from your breakthrough!

Chapter 2 Review

The Keys to Intercession

1. The acronym PUSH stands for "Pray _Until_ Something _Happen_."
2. Intercessory prayer is a _High_ calling.
3. God is seeking for somebody that will remind Him of His _Promises_
4. Sometimes intercessory prayer will cause you _To Cry_ before the Lord.
5. As an intercessor, you will _Plead_ the case of another before the _Throne_ of God.
6. Certain situations will require us to ~~Easy~~ _Turn_ our ~~plans~~ plate down and turn our _Faces Faces_ to the wall.
7. Intercessors come _Bodly_ to the throne of God and they make _requests_ according to their covenant promises. _- Petitions_

What tugs on your heart the most? For whom should you be interceding?

My Husband, Children,
Family, Pastors, Churches
Leaders, Nation, ~~People~~
Property, abortions,
People Minds,
✱ Spiritual growth
that People will be
intentional to take
responsibility for their
growth.

What Goes Up, Must Come Down

Bridgette's head hung down as she stood by the bus stop waiting for her father to come and pick her up from school. Once he arrived, he noted that she was visibly sad.

The drive home was quiet. Her dad made small talk inquiring how her day at school had gone. "fine," she responded.

After they arrived home, Bridgette rushed off toward her room. Her daddy stopped her asking if there was anything she wanted to talk about.

She looked up at him with beautiful brown eyes no, filled with tears. She began sobbing inconsolably, "Daddy, I didn't make the track team. Can you make me faster?"

Her father, filled with compassion, reached out gently and pulled her to his side assuring her "Yes, I will show you how."

"If you then, being evil, know how to give good gifts to your children, how much more will your Father who is in heaven give good things to those that ask him" Matthew 7:11.

In the succeeding pages we will discuss the power of prayer for I believe God is raising effective and fervent prophetic intercessors. We will look at several examples of intercessors throughout this book.

I have discovered in times of spiritual warfare, we as believers sometimes need to retreat before advancing. For example, in military vernacular, when the enemy is coming hard against troops, generals sometimes say, "I want you to retreat a little bit and get some reinforcement" After assessing the situation, receiving further instructions, they advance against their enemy.

I want to direct your attention to Daniel 10:10-13, which reads as follows:

> *10 Suddenly, a hand touched me, which made me tremble on my knees and on the palms of my hands.*

> *11 And he said to me, "O Daniel, man greatly beloved understand the words that I speak to you, and stand upright, for I have been sent to you." And while he was speaking this word to me, I stood trembling.*

> *12 Then he said to me, "Do not fear, Daniel, for from the first day you set your heart to understand, and to humble yourself before your god, your words were heard; and I have come because of your words."*

> *13 "But, the prince of the kingdom of Persia withstood me 20 and 1 days; and behold,*

Michael, one of the chief princes, came to help me, for I had been left alone there with the kings of Persia."

Consistency in prayer energizes and activates angelic involvement to fight off demonic and satanic hindrances and interferences. The Prince of Persia, in the verse twelve, is a principality over the region assigned to hinder, delay, or deny breakthrough.

The principle gleaned from this passage is that **Prayer is the Master Key**. More specifically your words in prayer. Here we see a universal law that teaches us that "what goes up, must come down" no matter how long it takes. It also reveals that delays are not necessarily denials, but can often signify spiritual warfare as in the case of the intercessor, Daniel. His prayers went up to God, and twenty and one days later, his answers were personally delivered by none other than the angel, Gabriel, after the angelic intervention of the Arch Angel Michael, who fought off the principality.

There was warfare in the spirit realm as the principality tried to keep the angel from getting through to Daniel with God's answer. The war was so intense that the angel Michael had to come and take Gabriel's place so that he could deliver the message.

Revelation 8:3-5 *"3 And another angel came and stood at the altar, having a golden censer; and there was given unto him much incense, that he should offer it with the prayers of all saints upon the golden altar which was before the throne.[4] And the smoke of the incense, which came with the prayers of the saints, ascended up before God out of the angel's hand.[5] And the angel took the censer, and filled it with fire of the altar, and cast it into the earth: and there were voices, and thunderings, and lightnings, and an earthquake."*

The word of the Lord teaches us according to Revelations 8:3-5, that the smoke of incense, which is the prayers of the saints, goes up into heaven.

According to the Old Testament, incense is a typology of prayer. When the priest of God burned incense at the Altar of Incense in the tabernacle of the Most-High God, it signified the prayers of the people of God. The Bible says that the smoke of incense, which is the prayers of the saints, goes up before God out of the angel's hands. The angel takes the golden censer and he fills it with fire from the altar and throws it to the earth; this is followed by sounds of thunder, flashes of lightening and finally an earthquake.

How exciting it is to learn that our intercessory prayers go from the earth realm to the heavenly realm escorted personally by God's angels which act as altar attendants. Yes, the angels become heavenly conduits taking our prayers and our praises before the Lord. Glory to God!

You are probably asking, what does all this intercessory prayer mean? It simply means that there must be an intercessor between heaven and earth. When there is no intercessor active in the earth realm, there are spiritual ramifications. For example, during the time of the Judges, Israel went through cycles where they wavered between loyal obedience and total rebellion. As a result, they ceased communication with God and the heavens were closed.

First Samuel chapter 3 reveals that Israel had no vision, which signifies they had no open heaven and God did not reveal Himself then. I have discovered that when the believer is walking in defeat it is due to them being spiritually bankrupt. What I mean by this can be summed up by a little saying I love to quote: "No relationship no power; no power, no anointing; no anointing, then you are vulnerable to the attacks of the enemy."

I do not know about you, but when my prayer life is lacking it seems that everything around me begins to shut down. However, when I am consistently in prayer with God, He opens the heavens on my behalf and grants me the desires of my heart. I have learned that when prayers go up, answers come down.

Let's look at another example of a woman named Hannah who understood the principal of prayer. You can find her story in the book of I Samuel chapters 1 and 2. It opens by introducing Elkanah, and his wives: Hannah (whose womb the Lord had shut) and Peninnah (who was fruitful). In other words, Hannah could not have children and Peninnah could.

Hannah was so mocked and ridiculed by Peninnah that even after her husband reaffirmed his love for her and her worth to him, it still didn't satisfy Hannah's heaviness of heart drove her to the only one that could help, her God. Thus, Hannah prayed and pleaded with the Lord making a vow unto Him saying these words:

> *"Oh Lord of Heaven, if you will look down on my sorrow and answer my prayer and give him a son, then I will give him back to you and he will be yours his entire life time and his hair will never be cut" (I Samuel 1:11)*

And as she was praying, the Bible reveals that her prayers were so intense that the priest, Eli, interrupted her, mistaking her body language for that of a drunk woman:

Sometimes when we are travailing before the Lord, we can be easily misunderstood, but we must press on. Many of us would falter in the face of such persecution and mean-spirited people, but Hannah preserved until Heaven opened and she got her answer.

The Bible reveals that God answered Hannah's prayer by giving her a male child. She dedicated her first born son Samuel to God and raised up a prophetic intercessor for the nation of Israel.

My friend, God so longs to give us the deep desires of our hearts according to His word (Psalms 37:4b). Hannah prayed for herself and God heard and answered her. She believed in the power of prayer and so God blessed her seed Samuel. He too believed in the power of prayer and was ordained a prophet and an intercessor on behalf of the Nation of Israel. Let's look at the intercessor Samuel in action in 1 Samuel 7:7-10.

7 And when the Philistines heard that the children of Israel were gathered together to Mizpeh, the lords of the Philistines went up against Israel. And when the children of Israel heard it, they were afraid of the Philistines.8 And the children of Israel said to Samuel, "Cease not to cry unto the Lord our God for us, that he will save us out of the hand of the Philistines."9 and Samuel took a sucking lamb, and offered it for a burnt offering wholly unto the Lord: and Samuel cried unto the Lord for Israel; and the Lord heard him.10 And as Samuel was offering up the burnt offering, the Philistines drew near to the battle against Israel: but the Lord thundered with a great thunder on that day upon the Philistines, and discomfited them; and they were smitten before Israel.

This passage of scripture shows Samuel crying out to God on behalf of Israel as the Philistines were coming against them. God answers with thunder, discomforting and confusing them, and the Israelites were able to chase them down and kill many. When Samuel prayed, God heard and delivered His people. What goes up must come down. Are you sending your prayers up to God?

Chapter 3 Review
What Goes Up, Must Come Down

1. Our intercessory _____ go
   from the earth realm to the _____ realm
   escorted personally by God ____._____

2. Hannah's first born son's name was _____
   and he was called to intercede on behalf of _____
   _____

3. Who was Hannah's rival?_____

4. What did she do to Hannah?_____

5. Does God always answer?_____

6. In times of spiritual warfare, we as believers
   sometimes need to _____before
   advancing.

7. No relationship, no _____; no power, no _
   _____; no anointing, then you are vulnerable
   to the attacks of the _____.

JOURNALING
WHAT COMES UP, MUST COME DOWN

Reflect on ways that God has already answered prayer in your life.

_____

_____

_____

_____

_____

_____

_____

_____

_____

_____

_____

_____

_____

_____

_____

_____

Chapter 4

Enlisting Spiritual Snipers

In the criminal world, we have levels of law enforcement. Such representatives consist of local, state and federal agencies: FBI, CIA, National Guard, local police officers and S.W.A.T. Teams (special weapons assault team) are usually called in during hostage situations, terrorist threats, bomb threats, hijackings, complex bank robberies and when our national security is threated. Their primary objective is to find a way of entry so that they may strike their intended mark. They surround the target so that they cannot escape, look for a clear shot, and/or opportunity to apprehend the terrorist and to take them out.

Every agency is not required to be present at all crime scenes. Typically, police are the first line of defense. It is only after they have assessed the matter and determined that they need additional back up that they will call the next level of defense. The level of criminal activity will dictate which specific law enforcement agency is to be summoned.

If the world has a line of defense for criminal activity, so does the believer. However, we must be wise and understand who our enemies are and who we are fighting. The Bible tells us in Matthew 11:12b,

12 The Kingdom of Heaven suffereth violence and the violent taketh by force. (KJV)

12 The Kingdom of Heaven has been forceful advancing, and forceful men lay hold on it. (NIV)

The Kingdom of Heaven is a spiritual realm and therefore the violence committed is spiritual. Intercessors, we are fighting spiritual criminals in this battle. We need to know which line of defense is necessary for each assignment that we are given. Second Corinthians 10:3-6 sheds light on this:

3 For though we walk in the flesh, we do not war after the flesh. 4 For the weapons of our warfare are not carnal, but mighty through God to the pulling down of strongholds, 5 casting down imaginations, and every high thing that exalts itself against the knowledge of God, and bringing into captivity every thought to the obedience of Christ, 6 and having a readiness to revenge all disobedience, when your obedience is fulfilled.

The members of the law enforcement agencies listed in beginning of this chapter had to be able to perform certain skills their respective missions. They had:

1. Obey their commander's voice
2. Follow Him
3. Be skilled with their weaponry
4. Participate in intense training
5. Sacrifice personal agendas
6. Have the heart to destroy their enemy
7. To know their enemy

Likewise, in the spiritual realm certain battles require different levels of spiritual defense and plans of enforcement. We are called to be spiritual snipers. What is required of the Spiritual Sniper, you may ask.

When a sniper sees his target, he cannot afford to miss. Say to yourself out loud, "I can't afford to miss." Even if you have been hitting and missing for the past few years, say to yourself, "But, today a new anointing comes upon me and I will never miss again because I've been called to be a spiritual sniper."

When we become familiar and acquainted with the tricks and the devices of the enemy, we can prayerfully plan our strategy and be on guard for his subtle and not so subtle attacks.

We must first position ourselves to guard our minds as intercessors, because that is the first place the enemy attacks. If he can keep your mind on petty things, then you won't have the mind to pray. If you don't have your mind stayed on God, you won't be in His perfect peace. Isaiah 26:3 *"³ Thou wilt keep him in perfect peace, whose mind is stayed on thee: because he trusteth in thee."*

The opposite of peace is confusion.

So the intercessor must be wise in the following areas:

1. Must know the voice of their commander and follow him. In John 10:24 Jesus says, *"My sheep hear My voice and I know them and they follow Me."*

2. Must be skilled with their weapon.
   And the helmet of salvation and the sword of the spirit which is the word of God. (Ephesians 6:17)

3. Must participate in intense training.
   And every man that strives for the Mastery is temperate in all things. Now they do it to obtain a corruptible crown, but we an incorruptible crown. I therefore so run, not as uncertainty; so fight I, not as one that beateth the air, but I keep under my body and bring it into subjection lest that by any means when I have preached to others, I myself should be a castaway.
   (1 Corinthians 9:25-27)

4. Must sacrifice personal agendas.
   Brethren, I count not myself to have apprehended: but this one thing I do, forgetting those things which are behind, and reaching forth unto those things which are before, I press toward the mark for the prize of the high calling of God in Christ Jesus. (Philippians 3:13)

5. Must have the heart and willlingness to destroy their enemy.

   The Kingdom of Heaven suffereth violence and the violent taketh by force. (Matthew 11:12)

6. Must know their enemy

   Lest Satan should get advance of us; for we are not ignorant of his devices. (II Corinthians 2:11)

Parga-ing through Principalities:

The Hebrew word for intercession is parga which means "to strike the mark or hit the target." When you are an intercessor, you are called to parga; you are called to hit your target because it is a matter of life or death. The intercessor cannot afford to miss. Ephesians 6:12 tells us,

For we wrestle not against flesh and blood, but against principalities, against powers, against the rulers of the darkness of this world, against spiritual wickedness in high places."

This verse describes the spiritual hierarchy in the satanic realm as such:

1. Principalities – Supreme Powers
2. Powers – Authorities
3. Rulers of Darkness of this World
4. Spiritual Wickedness in High Places

The saints of God are in a constant state of warfare with the powers of darkness. One of our most valued weapons is intercessory prayer. We entered this war when we said yes to Jesus. Keep your weapons oiled and ready because you may have to use them at a moment's notice.

Chapter 4 Review

Enlisting Spiritual Snipers

1. Intercessors, we are fighting _____ criminals.

2. We are called to be spiritual _____

3. The Kingdom of Heaven _____ _____violence and the _____ taketh by _____

4. For though we _____in the flesh, we do not __ _____after the _____

5. Casting down _____, and every high _____ _____ that exalts itself against the _____ of God, and bringing into _____ _____every thought to the obedience of _____.

6. Jesus said, "My _____hear My _____ _____and I know them and they _____ _____Me."

7. For we wrestle not against _____ and blood, but against _____ of   the darkness of this _____against spiritual wickedness in high _____

JOURNALING
SPIRITUAL SNIPERS

Reflect on areas of your life where you need to be a Spiritual Sniper.

_____

_____

_____

_____

_____

_____

_____

_____

_____

_____

_____

_____

_____

_____

_____

_____

Chapter 5

Praying Under an Open Heaven

Laura drove up to her garage after a hard weary day at work only to discover that she didn't have her garage door opener nor the keys to her house. In order to get inside, she would have to go to the neighbors next door where she had left a spare key, but she couldn't move because of intense fatigue. She called her husband on her cell phone and to her surprise he said he was at home. "What a relief!" she sighed. The garage door opened and as she pulled inside, he popped his head out of the kitchen door; and oh, what a feeling of warmth came over her.

One look at her told him how she felt, so he scooped her up in his arms and carried her through the open door to her favorite chair to rest.

That is the way it is with prayer and intercession. How wonderful it is to see heaven open up to us in the spirit when we press while praying and interceding.

Hebrews 3:1 says that Jesus is our High Priest and Apostle and that he is an always intercessor.

Luke 3:21 states that after he was baptized by John the Baptist signifying his death, burial and resurrection, Jesus came up from the water praying. **He came up from the water praying.** The Bible didn't say he came up from the water worshiping or praising but *praying*, and *then* the Heavens opened.

Jesus in this passage was being inaugurated into his calling as intercessor in the flesh for which I am eternally grateful. Thank you, Jesus! He is our example and what he did, we are to do. He stood in the gap and is calling us to do the same. I believe that God is challenging the body of Christ to intercede now like never before to link up in the spirit that we might pull down the strongholds of the enemy!

Christ has been my intercessor and I am grateful. He has and continues to intercede on my behalf. My friend, the prophets, priests, disciples, handmaidens, menservants, and every person called of God understood the essential purpose of prayer. Prayer is awesome and it is the Master key to our victory.

What is the key? Again a key is an instrument designed to unlock a door. In fact, prayer is the key that each believer must possess in order to unlock their doors of purpose. You must know that prayer is not a task that we opt to do; it is not optional; it is a mandate; it is a command. *"Men must always pray and not cease."* (Luke 18:1)

There are many areas that only the key of prayer will unlock:

1. Your Destiny
2. Your Purpose
3. Your Joy
4. Your Peace
5. Your Healing
6. Deliverance

7.   Your Revelations

We are able to see how each of these doors were opened as a result of praying and parga-ing in the chart below:

Scripture	Door to Unlock	Mark/Results
Num. 11:2; 21:7	God's Judgement	Repentance
1st Chron. 4	Child Abuse	Vindication
Ezra 10:1	Generational Curses	Blessings
Acts 16:16	Prison Doors	Paul and Silas free
Daniel 6:10	Revelations	Daniel received favor
Job 42:10	Deliverance	Friends
Acts 3:6	Lame	Healing

What doors in our life do you need unlocked? When we enter into prayer, we begin a relationship which is reciprocal. Prayer comprises of talking and listening. We, too, have to learn to be still and know that God IS. And that *He is a rewarder of them that diligently seek Him. (Hebrews 11:6)* Once we mature in a lifestyle of prayer, then God quickens us to begin to hear His voice.

As I travel around the world, I have found that believers all over this globe are seeking God concerning their destiny. Saints want to know the answers to those age old questions, "What is my purpose and future? What does tomorrow hold for me?" I am so glad that the Bible tells us that God will unlock our future, if we would only pray. He says in Jeremiah 29:11,

"For I know the plans I have for you and the thoughts I think towards you, they are good and not evil they are to give you a hope an expected end."

God thinks often of the saints and has prepared great and wonderful gifts for us. He says in 1 Corinthians 2:9,

"But as it is written, "Eye hath not seen, nor ear heard, neither have entered into the heart of man the things which God hath prepared for them that love him."

The Spirit gives revelation as He wills according to Daniel 2:22, *"He revealeth the deep and secret things: He knoweth what is in the darkness, and the light dwelleth with Him."* I believe that the throne room of His presence as we consistently and persistently seek His face.

The throne room is where we begin to train ourselves to recognize and know the voice of God. John 10:14 says, "I am the Good Shepherd, and know my sheep, and am known of mine." People of God, let our prayers rise as incense before the throne of God that the heavens will be opened, and when the heavens are open thunder ad lightening will descend. You need to understand that thunder and lightning are a sign that rain is coming. When you see the heavens change in the spirit and the clouds begin to get dark, when you begin to hear thunder in the distance and see lightening sniping, you know that rain is about to come. I must tell every reader that I hear the sound of an abundance of rain. Hallelujah!

Elijah said, "I hear the sound of the abundance of rain!" He told Ahab to get in his chariot and go quickly down the mountains and Elijah began to run. It is about to rain in your family; it is about to rain upon your children; it is about to rain in your ministry; it is about to rain in your home; it is about to rain in your business. I hear the sound of abundance! I hear the sound of abundance! The rain is coming. The Heavens are open!

One night I called my friend Barbara in Bellflower and as I was talking to her she said with great rejoicing, "Sister Sarah, it's raining over here in Bellflower!"

I said, "Where is the rain over here? I don't see any rain in Inglewood." My friend, I have come to tell you, if you can pray and if you can parga and strike the mark, it could rain right where you are. I prayed and before the night was over, it began to rain in Inglewood too. I'm telling you, "What goes up, must come down."

1. There are many areas that only the key of _____ will unlock.

2. Prayer consists of _____ and _____ _____. We too have to learn to be still and know that God is. And that he is a rewarder of them that diligently seek him.

3. Eye hath not Seen _____, nor ear _have_ heard, neither have entered into the _____ _____, the things which God hath prepared for hem that _____ him.

4. Prayer is awesome and it is the _____ to our victory.

5. For I know the _____ I have for you and the thoughts I think towards you, they are good and not evil they are to give you a _____ and an _ _____ end.

6. When you have an open _____ you will hear the voice of God.

7. Elijah said, "I hear the sound of the _____ of rain!" He told Ahab to get his chariots and he began to _____.

JOURNALING
PRAYING UNDER AN OPEN HEAVEN

Pray to God for an Experience of Prayer Under an Open Heaven.

_____

_____

_____

_____

_____

_____

_____

_____

_____

_____

_____

_____

_____

_____

_____

Chapter 6

The Character of an Intercessor

Pastor Sylvia was a strikingly beautiful woman of God who pastored a congregation primarily made up of college students. She believed firmly in intercessory prayer and led her young congregation in many all-night prayer vigils.

A local college football team attended her weekly prayer meetings. Jim, a handsome, tall, powerfully built linebacker frequently attended, but with ulterior motives. He was very attracted to Pastor Sylvia and he let her know on several occasions.

Fully aware of Jim's feelings, she made sure she was never alone with him; students were always around and when she met with him, it was always in a group sessions.

Over a period of time, Pastor found herself being attracted to him also. She ended up having a short intimate relationship with him.

When she finally confessed to her pastoral colleague, her excuse was "it happened so fast." Her colleague responded, "I could have been interceding for you."

Accountability is essential in the believer's life. God never called the man or woman of God to handle temptations alone. Our wonderful Father also encourages us to confess faults, weaknesses, and temptations one to another and pray for one another that we might be healed. *The effectual fervent prayer righteous man availeth much. (James 5:16 KJV).* As we carefully examine the next scripture in Titus we find that the man or woman of God must walk circumspectly in their calling. In the book of Titus, chapter 1 verses 7-9, Apostle Paul the character standard and requirement for ministry leaders:

7 Theses pastors must be men of blameless lives because they are God's ministers. They must not be proud or impatient, they must not be drunkards, or fighters, or greedy for money.

8 They must enjoy guest in their homes and must love all that is good. They must be sensible men, and fair. They must be clean minded and level headed.

9 Their belief in the truth which they have been taught must be strong and steadfast, so that they will be able to teach it to others and show those that disagree with them where they are wrong.

The intercessors should possess all the aforementioned characteristics described for ministry leadership. The following traits however, should not be named amongst them:

- Gossiping (II Corinthians 12:20)
- Slandering (Proverbs 18:8)
- Judging (Matthew 7:1)

- Respecter of Person (Acts 10:34)
- Gluttony (Proverbs 23:2)
- False Witness (Psalms 63:11) (Proverbs 19:5)
- Slothfulness (Proverbs 6:2)
- Exaggerating (Proverbs 6:2)
- Grossness (II Peter 2:12)

The intercessor must guard his or her tongue that it will not be used for the enemy's glory. Titus 1:10-13 admonishes us this way:

10 For there are many unruly and vain talkers and deceivers, especially they of they ought not, for filthy lucre sake.
11 Whose mouths must be stop, who subvert whole houses, teaching things which they ought not, for filthy lucre sake.
12 One of themselves, even a Prophet of their own, said, "Cretans are always liars, evil beasts, slow bellied."
13 This witness is true. Wherefore rebuke them sharply, that they may be sound in the faith.

Character is vital to God. He is not so concerned with what we do, say, how eloquent we pray, but the condition of our hearts. The scripture tells us, *"Out of the abundance of the heart the mouth speaketh." (Matthew 12:34b)*

I believe that your Gift dictates your Potential, but your charater determines your Legacy. A gift is given, but character is developed. Your character will get you in, but it is your charater that keeps there.

Chapter 6 Review

The Character of an Intercessor

1. God never called the man or woman of God to handle _____ alone.

2. Accounting is _____ in the believer's life of intercession.

3. Deuteronomy 33:30 teaches the believer that "one could put a _____ to flight and two _____."

4. The intercessor must also _____ and _____ their tongues that they are not used for the _____ glory.

5. Name some activities that Intercessors should not be involved in:

   _____, _____, _____, _____
   _____, _____, _____, _____
   _____

6. Name some character traits of an Intercessors:

   _____, _____, _____, _____
   _____,

7. Titus 1:10 says, "For there are many _____ and _____ talkers and deceivers, specially they of the _____

JOURNALING
MY CHARACTER

Reflect on the particular traits that you need to develop as an intercessor:

_____

_____

_____

_____

_____

_____

_____

_____

_____

_____

_____

_____

_____

_____

Chapter 7

The Posture of an Intercessor

3 Who shall ascend into the hill of the Lord? Or who shall stand in his holy place?

4 He that hath clean hands, and a pure heart; who hath not lifted up his soul unto vanity, nor sworn deceitfully.

5 He shall receive the blessing from the Lord, and righteousness from the God of his salvation.

6 this is the generation of them that seek him, that seek thy face, O Jacob. Sehah. (Psalms 24:3-6)

Posturing is very Key in the Intercessor's life. Monitoring our posture is an act of great wisdom. There are three distinct postures that the Intercessor must be careful to take:

1. Humility
2. Mercy
3. Pleader

Humility – God is looking for the humble that he may exalt. As intercessors, we are not to be prideful and boasters in our positions. First Peter 5:6 says, *"Humble yourselves therefore under the mighty hand of God, that he might exalt you in due time."*

We have to remember that our prayers are what God commands us to do, but the glory goes to God. We have too many intercessors exalting themselves based on God's answer to their prayers. We must remember it's the not the one who prays that makes the different, but the one who listens and answers. Intercessors please stay humble before the Lord. Jesus taught his disciples the key to staying humble when he exhorted them in this way:

"And when thou pray, thou shall not be as the hypocrites are; for they love to pray, standing in the synagogues and in the corners of the streets, that they may be seen of men. Verily I say unto you, they have their reward. But, thou, when thou pray, enter into thy closet, and when thou has shut thy door, pray to the Father which is in secret; and thy Father which see in secret shall reward thee openly. " Matthew 6:5-6

The principle for he scripture shouts: As an intercessor, let us resist going before God with pride, arrogance and presumption! History shows that God hates a prideful look and a haughty spirit. Lucifer learned this lesson best in Isaiah 14:12-15:

12 "How art thou fallen from heaven, O Lucifer, Son of the morning. How art thou cut down to the ground, which did weaken he nations!

*13 For thou has said in thine heart, 'I will ascend
into heaven, I will exalt my throne above the stars
of God;*
*14 I will ascend above the heights of the clouds; I
will be like the Most High.*
*15 Yet thou shall be brought down to hell, to the
sides of the pit."* (KJV)

Mercy – The Word of God says that on the day that
Jesus died, there were two robbers on both sides of him.
One looked at him and realized that this must be the Son
of the Living God. The Sinless Lamb he thought,
"Maybe I can get to heaven after all." He said to Jesus,
"Remember me when you come into your kingdom."
Jesus, being a merciful and longsuffering God, not
willing that any should perish, agreed. He looked on the
thief and said, "Today, you will be with me in paradise."
The Living Word interceded on behalf of the thief and
the same day walked with him in paradise.

Has compassion departed from the church of the
living God? Let us not think more highly of ourselves
that we ought, Church. Let us not be so "holier than
thou" that we can no longer identify with the adulterers,
the fornicators, the homosexuals, the drug addicts, and
those bound by sin and wickedness. May we be like the
intercessor Nehemiah, who included himself in the
repenting prayer that he prayed on behalf of his nation.
Instead of praying, **"Lord, forgive them,** "he prayed,

"Lord, forgive us." He understood that but for the grace of God where would I be?"

Pleader (7 categories) – Isaiah 43:26b invites us to come and *"...let us plead together...."* We are invited to plead with the Lord on our behalf and on the behalf of others. "Plead your case before me," He says. God loves healthy discussions and I am glad He allows me to do that. I am glad, He opens the door for all my requests.

The Hebrew word for "plead" is s***haphat***: to contend, reason, beseech, appeal, petition before God. Remember Hannah's prayer in Chapter 2. Her prayer is an example of pleading before God: *"Oh Lord of Heaven, if you will look down on my sorrow and answer my prayer and give me a son, then I will give him back to you and he will be yours his entire life time and his hear will never be cut."*

In my time with the Lord, He has revealed to me 7 categories in which the intercessor can plead unto Him:

1. **Plead the Honor and Glory of His Name.**
    When approaching God, we should always remember that He is unlike anyone or anything that He is unlike anyone or anything else in the entire universe. He is glorious, and is most honorable and we should tell Him of His glory. When petitioning God, be willing to say, "Whatever you do, do it for your sake. Do it for your name sake: save my husband for your namesake; deliver my son for your namesake; set the people free for your namesake."

63

2. Plead God's Relationship to Us

Remind God of His relationships to us:

    a.   You are my creator

    b.   You are my Helper

    c.   You are my Redeemer

    d.   You are my Father

    e.   You are my Friend

3. Plead His Attributes

Declare before God His unique character traits: "You are awesome. You are righteous. You are faithful. You are a kind God. You are a merciful God. You are slow to anger and quick to forgive. You are a long-suffering God."

4. Plead the sorrows and the needs of the people

Tell God exactly what is going on. Resist the mindset of, "God already knows, why do I need to tell him?" Yes, God wants you to tell Him about the pain, the sorrow, the sickness, the infirmity, the affliction, and the hunger that is going on in the lives of His people.

5. Plead the Past Answers to Prayers

Remind God that He is the same yesterday, today, and forever and He never changes (Hebrews 13:8 KJV). He delivered you before and He will do it again. Speak those things out!

You are the same God that brought me out of poverty; you are the same God that brought me out of poverty; you are the same God that dlivered me when I had no money; had no one, had no house, had no clothes. You can plead to God to do it again, Lord! Do it again! Do it again, Lord, for your name sake!

When Israel asked David, "How can you stand before Goliath?" David looked at the nation of Israel and he said, "The same God that killed the bear is the same God that will deliver me from the hands of the enemy." David was persuaded that God cold do it again!

6. Plead the Word and the Promises of God

As an intercessor plead the word of God and the promises of God. In Him, His promises are Yes and Amen! You can tell God, "I thank You, Lord, that according to 1 John 1:9, You said *if I confess my sins that you will be faithful and just to forgive my sin, and cleanse me of all unrighteousness*." And Lord, "I thank You that according to I Peter 2:24, *by your stripes I am already healed*." "Lord, I praise You that according to Psalm 103:3, *You have forgiven all of my iniquities and healeth all of my diseases*." Pray the promises and watch God move in your life.

7. Plead the Blood

God has given us power and authority through his Son's blood, the blood of the Lamb that was slain before the foundation of the world. When everything else fails, the blood never fails. The blood gives you the right to go before God knowing that every handwriting of ordinances that was against us was blotted out (Colossians 2:14 KJV).

When you go before God, have your homework done and approach Him in faith and understanding. You need to remind Him in faith and understanding. You need to remind Him of the blood that was wrapped in the womb of the Virgin Mary. The blood was beginning its redemptive work as he agonized and wrestled with principalities and powers in Gethsemane for your sins and for mind. His sweat was, as it were, great drops of blood falling to the ground (Luke 22:44b KJV).

Remind the Father of the agony of Gethsemane, remind the Father of the strong cries of the Son as he travailed for our salvation; remind the Father of the dark hour of Calvary. Glory to God

Chapter 7 Review

The Posture of an Intercessor

8. Name the three postures of an intercessor: 1. ___
   _____ 2. _____
   3. _____

9. Psalm 24:3 says, "Who shall _____ into
   the ___

10. Of the Lord? Or who shall _____
    in His holy place?"

11. 1 Peter 5:6 says, "_____yourselves
    therefore under the mighty _____
    _____ of God, that he might _____you   in
    due time."

12. We must remember that it isn't we who pray that
    makes the real difference, but He who _____
    _____ and _____

13. The Hebrew word for "plead" is _____

14. Describe the power of the Blood of Jesus.

Name the 7 components of a Pleader:

1. _____
2. _____
3. _____
4. _____
5. _____
6. _____
7. _____

JOURNALING
MY POSTURE

I need to grow in my posture in the following areas:

_____

_____

_____

_____

_____

_____

_____

_____

_____

_____

_____

_____

_____

_____

_____

Chapter 8

Releasing the Intercessor in You

Recently there was a story in the news about a fatal car accident. While racing down the freeway, Bob and Ray tragically ran into another vehicle. The truck that they hit immediately burst into flames. They got out, looked at the inflamed car, heard the trucker crying out for help and fled the scene.

Can you picture that? They didn't even try to assist him. He continued calling out until he finally found something heavy enough to break the window and quickly crawled away to safety. By then, the truck had become a burning inferno and shortly after his exit, it exploded. The trucker got out just in the nick of time. Still, he had third degree burns over two-thirds of his body all because there was no one to help.

How could Bob and Ray have been so heartless you ask? Well, let me ask you a questions, is someone in hell today asking that same questions about you? Are they saying, "They knew the road I had taken and they did nothing to stop me. They fled the scenes of my life. I was warned once, but after that, they said, 'Oh, well, I told him and he has made his choice.' Surely, if someone had cared enough

69

*to lay before the Lord on my behalf, I would
have possible changes."*

God is calling the body of Christ to stand in the gap
for a lost and dying world on their way to a burning hell.
People will literally go into an eternally burning hell If
we do not choose to stop and take the time to pray them
into the Kingdom of God. That is putting a lot of
responsibility on me, you say. Surely, my interceding is
not that vital. Surely, it's not life eternal or death eternal
if I do not intercede. Well, man or woman of God, it is.
Let's look at what God has to say about the matter in
Ezekiel 22:31-32:

*31 "So, I sought for a man among them who
would make a wall, and stand in the gap before
me on behalf of the land, that I should destroy
it; but I found no one.
32 Therefore have I poured out my indignation
upon them. I have consumed them with the fire
of my wrath: their own way have I
recompensed upon their heads," said the Lord
God.*

The Father is looking for people to employ in the
arena of intercession. The ad reads as follows:

> **[Classified]**
> **WANTED**
> **Prophetic Intercessor**
>
> Must be committed, faithful, trustworthy and tenacious. Saints that understand the seriousness of the cause. Saints that are sold out to the Kingdom. Saints that will never back up. Saints that are willing to lay down their lives when called to do so. God is looking for such a people. Could that be you? Please submit your spiritual resume to the Spirit of the Living God. No experience Necessary. Will Train.

God is raising up prophetic intercessors whereby we pray with insight and advanced knowledge because we know the Word of Truth. We pray not only by insight and by the Word of God, but also by revelation and the prompting of the Spirit of the living God. When we spend time with Him, He will show us things to come; He will make us to understand the times and the seasons. We are friends of God, and because of that, He will show us stuff.

People of God, I am releasing a revelation to you even as He is calling you in this hour. We are living in perilous times and evil days. Satan is not so subtle any more. He is boldly manifesting in the earth realm saying, "Hey, look at me." Unfortunately, many in the church still cannot see or feel the urgency of the hour, but be assured that Satan's time is running out. The Word warns us to,

71

"Be sober; be vigilant; because your adversary the devil, as a roaring lion, walketh about, seeking whom he may devour. (1Peter 5:8 KJV)

Satan is illegal and he is not even trying to cover his deeds. People of God, rise up and fight the good fight, ready your weapons, the battle has been won, the victory is ours and all we have to do is take it. Take it! Take it by force! Remember, intercession should be a lifestyle. We are always on the lookout next assignment. We should ask the Lord, "Lord, who do I pray for next"

Intercessors, are you ready? The Kingdom of Heaven is waiting. The communities are at stake, your family's eternity is at stake, your church is at stake, and your leaders are at stake! God is listening and waiting for the intercessors to rise up and pray!

Ture intercession flows out of a heat of compassion contrition and desperation. When we are sympathetic, we are saying, "I see your situation, condition or circumstance, but I cannot do anything about it."

When we are empathetic, it means that you now put yourself in the shoes of that person and it is like whatever is happening to them is happening to you. So, when you are a true intercessor your heart cries for whoever you are praying for. Your heart is heavy and burdened for that person, family, community, nation, church or pastor. A true intercessor has a burden in his heart and he places himself in the stead of the person being prayed for. As the mother eagle pushes her young

72

out of the comfortable nest, releasing it to fly on its own, so God releases us to fly in the spirit realm of intercession.

People of God, we have been dependent on others to do the praying for us long enough. We must be more than hearers and receivers of the Word of God. God is calling us to graduate to being doers and proclaimers:

- No longer to follow, but to lead the prayer of faith.
- No longer dependent on someone else to pray for our concerns, but boldly praying prophetically the Word of God in our situations.
- No longer second-guessing God's love and our worthiness to get a prayer answered, but claiming the promises of God.

IT'S TIME TO FLY IN THE SPIRIT.

Chapter 8 Review

Releasing the Intercessor in You

1. God said in Ezekiel 22:30, "So I sought for a ___ _____ among them who would make a wall, and _____ in the gap before me on behalf of the land, that I should not destroy it; but I found _____

2. We pray not only by _____ and by the _____ but also by _____ and the prompting of the _____ of the living God.

3. True intercession _____ out of a heart of _____ and desperation.

4. We are _____ in _____ times and evil days.

5. A _____ intercessor has a _____ in their heart and they place themselves in the ___ _____ of the person being prayed for.

6. When we are empathetic, it means that you now put _____ in the shoes of that person and it is like whatever is happening to _____ _____ is happening to _____ _____.

7. According to the Word of God in Ezekiel 22:30-21. Why it is important that you intercede?_____
   _____

JOURNALING
MY RELEASE

I covenant to be God's intercessor and stand in the gap for:

_____

_____

_____

_____

_____

_____

_____

_____

_____

_____

_____

_____

_____

_____

Chapter 9

Intercessors' Hall of Fame

Every year Hollywood celebrates its winners for outstanding leading and supporting acting roles. The industry goes all out to showcase its best. The actors dress up in designer dresses, furs and exquisite diamonds worth millions. The men, to, are draped in their tailored tuxedos and designer attire: all this for one evening.

The next item on their agenda is an escorted walk down the famous red carpet leading to one of Beverly Hills' finest hotels to sit and eat the best cuisines awhile America watches.

After years of making money for the industry, you are awarded one of the highest honors in Hollywood; and that is none other than receiving your star on the Walk of Fame in a little city called Hollywood, California.

Your name is joined with the company of great actors such as Sidney Portier, Ciceley Tyson, Ruby Dee. Clark Gable, Johm Wayne, Marilyn Monroe, Denzel Washington, and thousands of others.

The walk of Fame insures that these actors will never be forgotten. Their best work has made an indelible imprint on our hearts. They achieved their reward with a star on Hollywood

Boulevard. Many up and coming actors are striving for this same mastery and accomplishment. They are perfecting their gifts, making daily sacrifices to get to the top and giving themselves wholly unto it.

The believer, too, will have a grand celebration and it is called the Marriage Supper of the Lamb. Who will be there? Those whose names are written in the Lamb's Book of Life: Those whose robes have been washed in the Blood of the Lamb.

Yes, there is a Hall of Fame for us too. We will dress in the finest clothes; the jewels that we will wear will have no equal on this earth and the Lord himself will be distributing the honors. We will not walk on red carpet, but streets of Gold. The gates will be made of pearls and the walls roundabout will be made of every fine jewel imaginable. Not only will we wear fine clothing, but we will have a brand new body. He will give us an incorruptible crown, one that cannot be destroyed. And he will say to every intercessor,

"Well done, thou good and faithful servant; you have been faithful over a few things, now come up a little higher, and let me make you rulers over many" (Matthew 25:21 KJV)

God has His own Hall of Fame and we see a partial list that He calls a cloud of witnesses in the book of

Hebrews the eleventh Chapter. You will find a list of prophetic intercessors who walked by faith and not by sight, believing the promise. And I can hear God exhorting them as he opens the Lamb's Book of Life saying:

- "Well done, Abraham for interceding for Lot while he was in Sodom and Gomorrah."
- "Well done, Moses, for being willing to leave the comforts of Pharaoh's palace in Egypt denying the pleasures of sin for a season to intercede on behalf of my people."
- "Well done, Joshua for leading the people through the Jordan River into the promised land of Canaan, and challenging them to stand for Me. You presented them with the choice to choose whom they will serve."
- "Well done, Samuel, for parga-ing on behalf of Israel when their enemies were hard on their trails."
- "Well done, Esther, for being willing to sacrifice your worldly crown as queen to intercede for my people, so that Haman's plot would not succeed."
- "Well done, Nehemiah, for leaving your safe place in the king's palace to go to Jerusalem, a city without walls, and a people in reproach, to rebuild my city and my people through prayer. You had a mind to work."

- "Well done, Apostle Paul, for teaching my people the importance of prayer in their daily walk."

Beloved, the list will continue to grow until the day of redemption when our Lord and Savior return's. I have some questions for you:

Will you accept *The Invitation to the Throne Room?*
Will you possess *The Keys to Intercession?*
Will you believe *What Goes up Must Come Down?*
Will you be *Enlisted as a Spiritual Sniper?*
Will you *Pray Under an Open Heaven?*
Will you maintain *The Character of an Intercessor?*
Will you stand in *The Posture of an Intercessor?*
Will you allow God to *Release the Intercessor in You?*
Will your name be listed in *The Intercessors' Hall of Fame?*

Chapter 10

A Prophetic Prayer for You

As I conclude this assignment, I have unction to pray for you and those that are precious in your life.

Father, in the name of Jesus, I pray that you will bless and anoint every reader holding this book! Father, I pray you would open the eyes of their understanding to truth and grace. Father, please stir up the intercessor in each of them causing them to cry aloud and spare not.

Jehovah God, I pray that you raise them up and set them on the walls of life as watchmen over their appointed territories and that they might *parga* in the spirit!

Precious Holy Spirit, you are Teacher. Teach your men and women how to *parga* and *shaphat* for their children and families, their communities, and their leaders. Teach them how to call out to you for the nations as the true intercessors of God.

Jehovah God, raise up lieutenants in the spirit, raise up captains in the spirit, raise up generals in the spirit and raise up your holy ambassadors to bring into captivity every high thing that exalts itself against the word of God.

I bind the spirit of prayerlessness; I bind the spirit of sluggishness; I bind the spirit of laziness; I bind the spirit of intimidation, doubt, fear and torment. By the power of the blood of Jesus, I release the spirit of intercession into your churches everywhere; into your ministries, mission fields, and auxiliaries. I release it into your deacons and teachers, maidservants and menservants, your elders, bishops and your high priest. Father, I thank you that you said I the last days you would pour out your spirit upon all flesh and that our sons and daughters would prophesy and our young men would see visions, and our old men would dream dreams. I release the spirit of boldness, the spirit of authority, the spirit of courage in the spirit, to prayer. I release the anointing upon theses, Go, and pray until something happens; pray until bondages are broken; pray until yokes of poverty are destroyed; pray until yokes of infirmities are healed; pray until yokes of afflictions are released and your people walk and go free.

We shall pray in the morning, the afternoon, in the evening; in the meantime, and in between time. When life is good and when life is not so good. Father, we shall call upon you as your children continuously and without ceasing.

Father, I pray that your people would operate under the blessings of an open heaven; that they will become more sensitive and attentive to hearing your voice. Lord God, take them to new levels of prayer. Father, raise up the prophetic intercessors today! I *parga* for my sisters and brothers. Oh God, I *shaphat* you concerning your intercessors in the name of Jesus. I thank you that through the blood of Christ every stronghold of resistance has been broken by the Power of the Blood of Jesus Christ!

Thank you that you are lining up your intercessors a round this world to take back by force that which the enemy has stolen. Father, I pray, make us a people like the Bereans who studied your word and knew your promises. Do it again, Lord! Father, I pray that you deliver us from our enemies like you did for Jehosophat when the Amonites and Moabites came against Judah. Do it again, Lord!

Father, we thank you that we, too, will obtain a good report through faith in Jesus' Matchless and Wonderful Name. Amen!

WHO IS AN INTERCESSOR?

- A watchman, one, who never keeps silent, reminds the Lord and gives him no rest until he establishes (Isiah 62:6-7)
- One who makes up the hedge and builds up the wall of protection in time of battle (Ezekiel 13:4-5)
- One who stands in the GAP between God's righteous judgment that is due and the need for mercy on the people's behalf.

Remember

Remember prayer is not an activity, prayer is not a function, prayer is a lifestyle that translates and transfers us to another dimension and expression of His glory. True intercession flows out of a heart of compassion, contrition and desperation, with a heart that pounds with suffering of others as though they were ours. God is an equal opportunity employer, and the ministry of prayer and praise is the job description of every priestly and prophetic intercessor. To *intercede* means to intervene or intercept between parties with a view to reconciling differences. To go between; I sought for an intercessor there was none. Hebrew word: ***Parga* – strike the mark.**

As an intercessor you are called to be a spiritual sniper, God's Mark's Man or Mark's Woman. God is counting on you to hit the target through your prayer.

Intercession is not the preoccupation of the zealous few; it is the highest calling and destiny of chosen people of God.

God bless you on your Journey,

Prophetess Sarah Morgan

Covenant Page

God says, "So I sought for a man/woman among he who would make a wall, and stand in the gap before me on behalf of the land, that I should not destroy it; but I found no one (Ezekiel 22:30 KJV)

1. I have read, *Prayer, The Master Key: Raising Prophetic Intercessors In times Like These.*
2. I covenant with God to walk as one of his intercessory prayer vessels.
3. I partner today with Prophetess Sarah Morgan in her international crusade to *"Raise up Prophetic Intercessors in Times Like These."*
4. I agree to pray for this God-sent ministry.
5. Name:_____DOB:_
   _____Address:_____
   _____City/State_____
   _____Zip:_____
   Email Address: _____
   _____Church Affiliation: _____
   _____Pastor(s)
   Name: _____
6. How long have you been saved: _____Reborn
   Date: _____
7. Please add me to your mailing list and inform me of any conferences and training seminars on Intercessory prayer.
8. Signature: _____Date:__